Level 2

The Nature Kid's Guide to
WILD MUSTANGS

DAVID ANDERSON

LP Media Inc. Publishing

For information address LP Media Inc. Publishing,
30012 Variolite St NW, Princeton MN 55371
www.lpmedia.org

Publication Data

Wild Mustangs
The Nature Kid's Guide to Wild Mustangs — First edition.

Summary: "Learn all about Wild Mustangs, the Nature Kid Way"
— Provided by publisher.

ISBN: 979-8-89818-158-1

[1. Wild Mustangs – Non-Fiction] I. Title.

Title: The Nature Kid's Guide to Wild Mustangs

CONTENTS

WILD AND FREE
DID YOU KNOW?
Mustangs can survive on less water than farm horses. Their bodies adapted to the dry American West.

Splash! A wild mustang races through a river.

Wild mustangs live in wide open spaces. They need room to roam and run. These horses live in dry, rugged places. It does not rain much there.

Mustangs find homes in deserts. They live in grasslands too. Some live in mountain valleys. These areas can be rocky and steep. Summer days get very hot. Winter nights can drop below freezing.

Fresh water is hard to find. Mustangs travel up to 30 miles to reach streams. They also find springs. They eat tough grasses. These grasses grow in dry soil. These hardy horses survive where few other animals can.

ROAMING RANGES

Howl! Wind blows across the land. A wild mustang runs free.

Wild mustangs live in ten western states. Most live in Nevada. About half of all wild mustangs call Nevada home.

Other herds live in Wyoming, Utah, and Oregon. More herds roam in Montana, Idaho, and Colorado.

These horses can travel up to 40 miles in one day. They move from low valleys to high mountain meadows searching for food and water.

Some herds have lived in the same area for over 100 years. They pass down what they know each generation.

MIGHTY MUSTANGS

Thunder! A herd of mustangs gallop across the open valley.

At the shoulder, a wild mustang stands about five feet tall. Horse height is measured in hands. Mustangs are 14 to 15 hands high. One hand equals four inches.

Most mustangs weigh between 700 and 900 pounds. That makes them a bit smaller than most domestic horses you might see on a farm.

From nose to tail, a mustang stretches about eight feet long. That's longer than your bed!

A mustang's heart weighs about eight pounds. That is about eight times heavier than a human heart!

BUILT TOUGH

DID YOU KNOW?
A mustang's hoof grows about one-third of an inch every month and never stops growing.

Splash! A wild mustang crosses the cold river. Its legs push through.

Mustangs have bodies made for tough living. Their hooves are hard like rocks. Each hoof is actually one big toe covered in thick **keratin**. Keratin is the same thing your fingernails are made of!

A mustang's coat changes with the seasons. In winter, it grows long and fluffy. This keeps them warm in freezing weather. In summer, the coat sheds to stay cool.

Their legs are strong and lean. Thick **tendons** act like springs when they run. Mustangs also have large nostrils that pull in lots of air.

SUPER
SENSES

Sniff! A wild mustang lifts it's head and sniffs the wind.

Mustangs have amazing senses. Their ears turn up to 180 degrees. Each ear moves on its own to catch sounds from all directions.

A mustang's eyes are very large. These big eyes let them see nearly 360 degrees. This helps them spot danger from almost anywhere.

Their sense of smell is powerful too. Mustangs use their noses to find water, recognize other horses, and even smell predators before they can see them.

Mustangs can hear sounds from up to 2.7 miles away and smell water from miles across the desert!

KICK BACK

Whomp! A wild mustang's hooves fly up behind it. It kicks wildly!

Mustangs use their legs to stay safe. Their back legs are very powerful. One kick can break bones, which keeps predators away.

Mustangs also bite when threatened. Their strong, sharp teeth can leave a painful bite!

Their coloring helps them stay safe too. Brown and tan coats blend into dry grasslands. This makes them harder to spot from far away.

A mustang's kick can hit with 2,000 pounds of force. That is strong enough to dent a metal door!

GRAZE DAYS

DID YOU KNOW?
Mustangs can eat around 25 different kinds of plants.

Chomp! A herd of wild mustangs munch tall prairie grass together.

Mustangs eat plants all day long. They spend up to 18 hours **grazing** each day! Grass is their main food, but they also eat shrubs and small bushes when grass is **scarce**.

In winter, food is harder to find. Mustangs dig through snow with their hooves. They eat bark and twigs when grass is gone.

Mustangs need lots of water too (but less than domestic horses). They need to drink about 5 to 10 gallons each day.

HORSE TALK

FUN
FACT!
Mustangs can recognize each other's voices from up to a mile away, even in a large herd!

Clomp! A stallion hears a distress call and races toward his herd.

Mustangs talk to each other in many ways. They make different sounds for different things. A loud whinny says hello. A soft nicker means come closer.

Their bodies speak too. When ears go flat back, it means stay away. Ears forward show interest. A raised tail signals excitement.

Mustangs also use their noses. They blow air through their nostrils to warn others. A loud snort tells the herd that danger is near. Squeals also send messages and can mean back off during arguments.

WATCH OUT

Sniff! A mustang sniffs the air, it smells a mountain lion is nearby.

Mountain lions hunt mustangs. They are their main predator in many areas. These big cats hunt alone. They hide and wait to attack.

Wolves also hunt mustangs in some places. A wolf pack works as a team. They chase tired or weak horses.

Bears can hunt young foals. Coyotes do too. Grizzly bears are very big. They can even hunt adult mustangs.

Mountain lions can leap 40 feet in one pounce. They lie in wait and will jump onto a mustangs back.

RUN FAST

Roar! A blaze faced wild mustang races across the open plains.

Mustangs run to stay safe. When danger comes, they bolt fast. A mustang can reach 35 miles per hour. This speed helps them escape most predators.

The herd runs together. Mares and foals stay in the middle. The **stallion** often runs at the back.

Mustangs watch for threats while grazing. If one spots danger, the whole herd takes off.

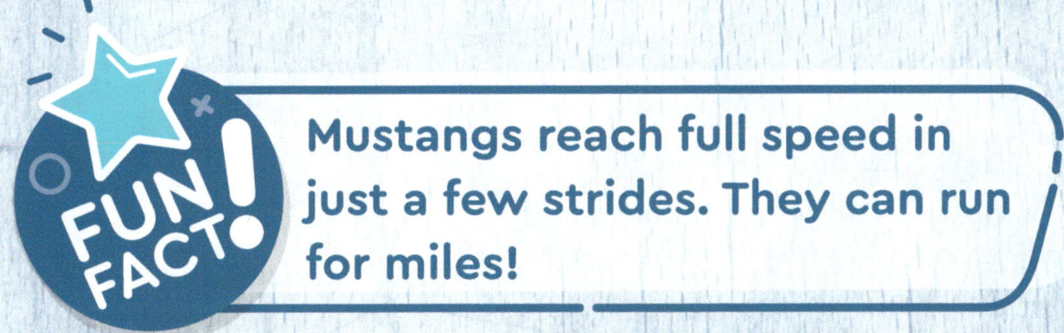

HERD LIFE

Sprint! A wild mustang runs back to his band.

Mustangs live in groups called bands. Each band has one stallion, several mares, and foals. Most bands have 3 to 12 horses.

The lead mare guides the band. She decides where to find food and water.

The stallion protects the band. He watches for danger and keeps the group together.

Young stallions leave their birth band around age two or three to join a bachelor band.

STALLION
SHOWDOWN

Smack! Two stallions clash in a dusty battle. Hooves pound the ground.

Mustangs usually mate in the spring and summer. Most foals are born in spring. This gives them warm weather to grow strong.

Stallions show off to impress mares. They arch their necks high, prance, and snort loudly.

Stallions also fight other males. They bite and kick until one wins. The winner keeps his band safe.

Mares carry babies for about 11 months. A newborn foal can stand and walk within one hour!

FUZZY FOALS

DID YOU KNOW?
Foals can run within a few hours of being born! This helps to escape predators!

Splash! A young foal drinks from a cool stream. Its mother watches nearby.

Baby mustangs are called foals. Most mares have one foal at a time, and twins are very rare.

Newborn foals have fuzzy coats. Their soft, fluffy fur keeps them warm in cool weather.

Foals are born with very long legs. Their legs look too big for their bodies! At birth, foals can weigh 60 to 100 pounds.

A foal's coat color may change as it grows. Many are born lighter and darken to their adult color.

MARE MOMS

Sip! A mustang mare drinks from a cool stream.

Mares are caring mothers. Wild mares feed their foals milk for about one year. But foals also start eating grass when they are just a few weeks old.

Mares teach foals important lessons. They show them where to find water and which plants are safe to eat.

Mares also protect their foals from danger. They keep them close in the herd.

Mares can recognize their own foal's whinny in a crowd of horses.

BORN SURVIVORS

32

Chomp! A mustang munches on dry grass. The hot sun shines down.

Wild mustangs have lived in North America for over 500 years. In the 1500s, Spanish explorers brought horses to America for the first time. They used them to travel and carry supplies across the land.

But some horses got loose. Others were left behind. These horses had to learn to survive on their own. They found wild grasses to eat and streams to drink from.

Over many years, their herds grew. They became the wild mustangs we see today.

VANISHING HERDS

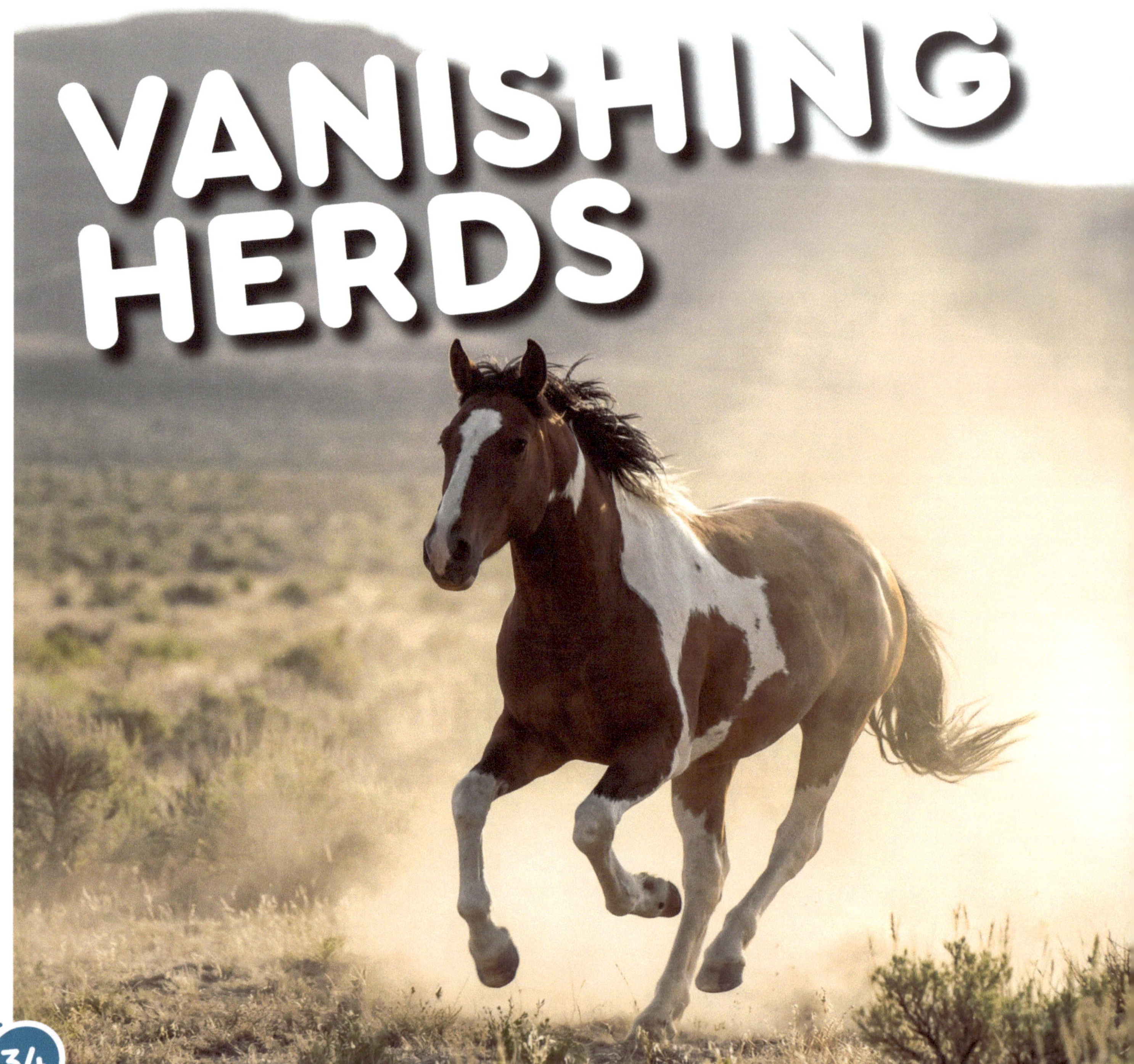

Click! Hooves tap the dusty ground as a mustang runs free.

At one time, millions of wild mustangs roamed across America. They ran free in big herds across the plains and deserts. But as more people moved west, things changed.

People built towns, roads, and fences on the land where mustangs lived. Ranchers wanted the grass for their cattle. Some people captured mustangs to use as work horses. Others hunted them for food.

By the 1970s, there were fewer than 20,000 wild mustangs left. Down from the millions that once roamed the United States.

SAVING
MUSTANGS

Hoot! An owl calls as a mustang dozes in the desert heat.

The wild mustangs needed help. In 1971, the United States government passed a special law to protect them. The law said that no one could hunt, capture, or hurt wild mustangs.

Since then, the herds have grown. Today, about 70,000 wild mustangs live in the western United States.

Wild mustangs are survivors. And with our help, they will keep running free across America.

Mustangs sleep only about three hours each day. They nap in short bursts to stay alert for danger.

SPOT THEM

Click! A camera snaps a photo. A wild mustang sprints across the desert!

Wild mustangs live in 175 Herd Management Areas. If you are visiting one of these areas, you may be able to spot one for yourself!

Stay at least 100 feet away. Use binoculars to see them up close. Never chase wild horses. Never feed them.

Watch quietly. Move slowly. If a horse pins its ears back, back away slowly and gently.

The best time to spot mustangs is early morning or evening. That is when they drink water.

GLOSSARY

keratin
A hard material that makes up hooves, fingernails, and hair.

tendons
Strong cords in the body that connect muscles to bones.

scarce
Not easy to find because there is not a lot of it.

grazing
Eating grass and plants that grow on the ground.

stallion
An adult male horse.